D0281555

DINOSAURS!

A FUN ACTIVITY BOOK FOR 6-12 YEAR OLDS

Hello!

Welcome to this super amazing book and thank you for purchasing (or if it's a gift and you're the recipient – thanks for reading!). You'll also soon be sketching, searching and solving, because this book is virtually brimming with fun activities to complete, all with a dinosaur theme!

So grab yourself;

A ballpoint

A pencil

A rubber

A ruler

A pair of eyes (preferably your own)

...and let's begin!

ANSWERS TO PUZZLES CAN BE FOUND AT THE END OF THE BOOK!

Your **name**

Your name if you were a
DINOSAUR

WHICH DINOSAUR APPEARS THE MOST?

Mirror
SAURS

Mirror
SAURS

MISSING T-REX

```
T R X E X X R E T X T R X E
E T R E T X E R E T X R E X
R T X E E T E R X T E E R T
T X E R X T R E T E X T R E
X E R E X T X T R T X E X R
T E R X T E E X E R R X E T
T R X E T R X X T E X R E X
X T E R E R T E R E X E T E
```

COLOUR THE
DINOSAURS!

OH NO.... VOLCANO!

Can you escape the explosion of hot lava?

COUNT the DINOSAUR EGGS!

Sketch Time!

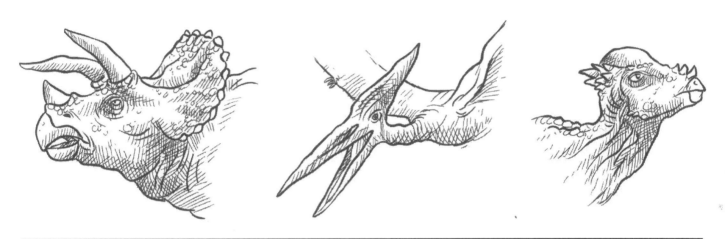

WHICH
DINOSAUR
IS WHICH?

PLESIOSAURUS
ALLOSAURUS
IGUANODON
ANKYLOSAURUS
PTERANODON
BRACHIOSAURUS
VELOCIRAPTOR
DEINONYCHUS

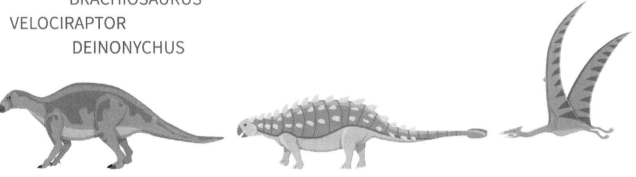

ALL THINGS DINOSAUR!

T	T	W	I	N	G	S	P	C	I	C	H	A	S
C	T	N	H	R	E	R	I	V	I	W	I	I	E
N	G	R	P	S	E	R	T	N	A	I	G	R	L
I	T	O	T	D	A	C	O	J	C	C	O	A	A
T	A	T	A	P	T	S	U	V	S	L	I	A	C
X	H	T	T	T	U	R	G	R	I	G	A	N	S
E	O	O	H	I	A	A	S	G	C	B	W	W	E
R	R	P	A	S	C	O	I	N	E	C	R	T	S
A	A	E	S	P	I	R	A	O	R	T	R	E	G
O	G	I	E	N	R	S	S	E	P	O	E	E	H
O	C	L	I	S	S	O	F	T	R	I	H	A	A
R	P	R	E	H	I	S	T	O	R	I	C	R	P
W	O	G	S	F	S	A	A	I	O	A	A	S	S
I	W	E	O	S	C	O	H	A	O	L	O	C	O

HORNS
RAPTOR
EGGS
GIANT
PREDATOR
ROAR
PREHISTORIC
FOSSIL
CLAWS
JURASSIC
WINGS
HERBIVORE
SCALES
EXTINCT

WHICH DINOSAUR APPEARS THE MOST?

Create your own
DINOSAUR!

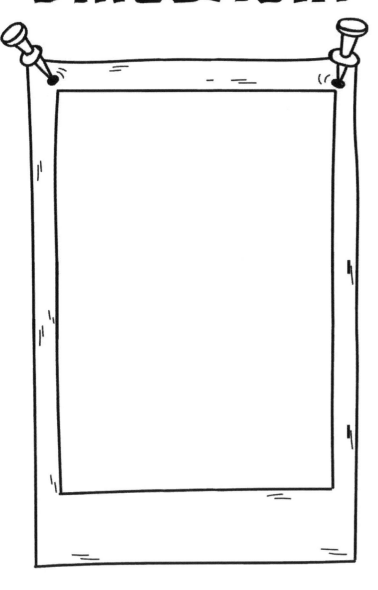

NAME

STRENGTHS

WEAKNESS

MAX
SPEED

THE TASTIEST TREE!

Help hungry Horris find the yummiest leaves around!

GRAB YOUR COLOURING PENCILS!

WHICH DINOSAUR GETS TO MEET THEIR TWIN?

SCRAMBLED!

Can you unscramble the dinosaur names?

SSALUAULRO

DOODCISUPL

YORNXAYB

OCAUSTARURN

IADNOUNGO

PICSTTOAERR

DROOANHTC

COMPLETE THE SKETCHES!

MATCH
THEN
RE-ATTACH!

Can you spot the **3 shadows** **without** a matching dinosaur?

DESIGN YOUR DREAM
DINOSAUR JUMPER!

TYPES OF DINOSAUR!

D	I	P	L	O	D	O	C	U	S	E	T	X	A
S	G	X	O	U	R	A	S	S	T	R	Y	R	S
T	U	Y	A	S	D	O	X	I	I	R	O	P	U
E	A	N	N	U	N	S	A	C	E	T	R	A	R
G	N	O	S	P	P	A	E	T	P	A	I	L	U
O	O	D	G	R	O	R	P	A	O	A	T	L	A
S	D	R	U	R	A	O	R	L	O	D	O	O	S
A	O	A	R	T	E	I	R	U	G	O	P	S	O
U	N	A	O	A	C	S	A	R	G	S	C	A	T
R	A	P	H	O	U	O	P	P	T	O	V	U	A
U	S	C	L	A	O	R	P	O	U	D	U	R	P
S	R	E	O	P	R	G	O	Y	O	R	X	U	A
A	V	S	U	R	U	A	S	O	N	I	P	S	C
P	N	O	R	G	I	R	A	U	X	R	O	N	R

ARCHAEOPTERYX
VELOCIRAPTOR
SPINOSAURUS
STEGOSAURUS
APATOSAURUS
RUGOPS
TRICERATOPS
IGUANODON
ALLOSAURUS
DIPLODOCUS
AARDONYX

D I N O   D O U B L E S !

A DINOSAUR HAS BEEN CAUGHT STAMPING ON SOMEONE'S HOUSE!

CAN YOU SPOT THE FOOT PRINT LOCATED AT THE SCENE OF THE CRIME?

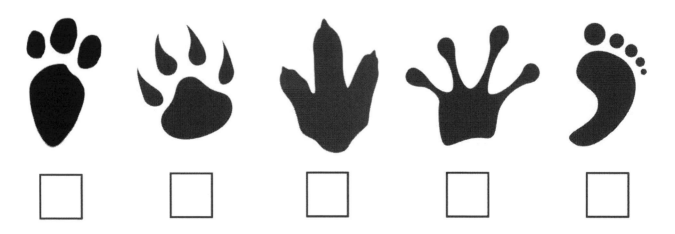

COLOURING
TIME!

Your TOP 5 favourite **DINOSAURS** (and why!)

1 _____   _____

2 _____   _____

3 _____   _____

4 _____   _____

5 _____   _____

WHICH SHADOW APPEARS THE MOST...

AND WHICH APPEARS THE LEAST?

Sketch Time!

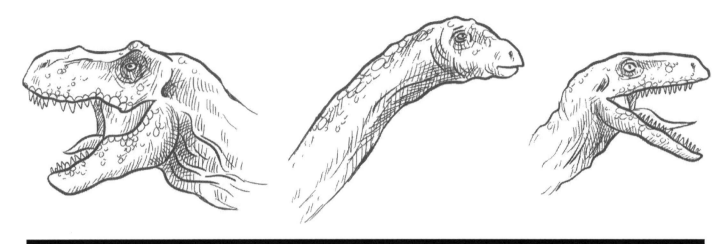

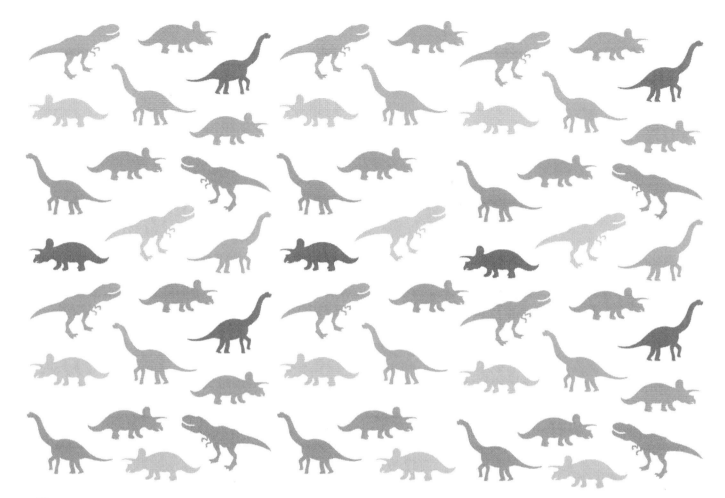

COUNT THE DINOSAURS!

GRAB YOUR **COLOURING PENCILS!**

Help newly hatched **Iggy** out of the maze!

FIND MY PARENTS!

MY DINOSAUR NAMES PAGE

Jot down your favourite names, ready for your new dinosaur pets and toys!

Mirror
SAURS

WHICH DINOSAUR APPEARS THE MOST?

GRAB YOUR COLOURING PENCILS!

WHERE'S MY TWIN?
Which route should he take?

A

B

C

WHICH DINOSAUR IS WHICH?

COLOUR THE **SCARY GODZILLAS!**

NAMES FOR DINOSAURS!

E	T	A	Y	R	M	O	E	R	H	S	A	T	B
G	C	M	S	E	E	T	R	P	T	Y	R	E	A
X	H	S	R	T	T	O	Y	R	O	R	Y	T	E
E	O	T	R	S	E	I	D	R	R	Y	R	N	S
I	M	N	E	E	H	G	B	R	O	I	T	Y	R
I	P	O	X	R	R	A	G	I	K	N	G	Y	A
S	U	E	G	R	T	I	M	E	X	R	E	O	S
P	S	M	L	R	O	X	Y	M	R	C	E	R	E
I	R	D	K	I	I	C	R	G	E	S	D	I	I
K	H	S	A	D	B	M	Y	S	D	R	W	B	P
E	T	T	P	R	Y	R	L	A	N	Y	I	T	H
D	A	R	O	T	P	A	R	E	R	E	N	R	R
S	E	Y	S	H	P	Y	E	R	Y	A	A	K	O
R	I	A	N	K	R	B	G	K	M	I	T	M	R

REX
RAPTOR
TYRONE
EDWINA
TRIKE
ROXY
CHOMPUS
DASH
BITEY
RORY
HAMMER
STEGGERS
SPIKE
GRIMLEY

WHICH WAY TO MY NEST?

Help Gertie back to her nest of eggs!

Sketch Time!

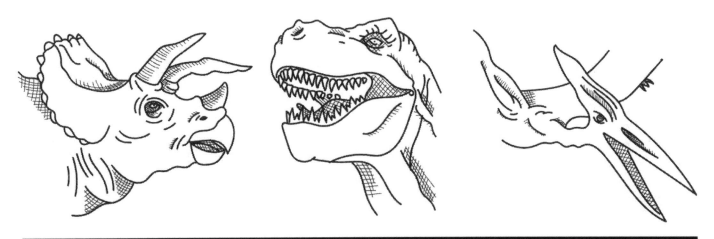

WHICH DINOSAUR APPEARS THE MOST?

GRAB YOUR
COLOURING
PENCILS!

EGG HUNT!

Can you help poor Dingo find his precious egg?

Create your own
DINOSAUR!

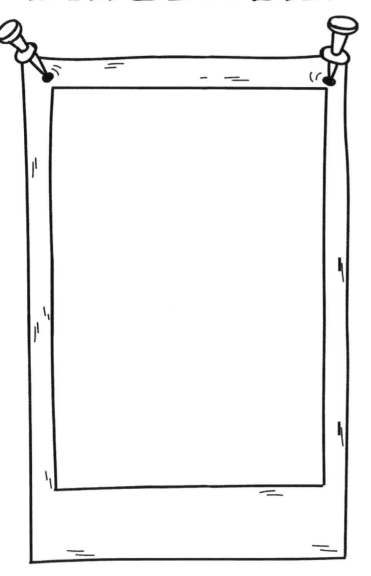

NAME

STRENGTHS

WEAKNESS

MAX SPEED

COMPLETE THE SKETCHES!

MATCH THEN RE-ATTACH!

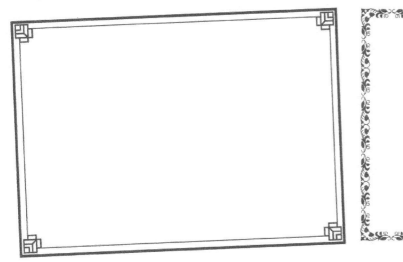

4 words to describe DINOSAURS!

COLOUR IN THE DINOSAURS!

WHICH DINOSAUR SHADOW APPEARS THE **MOST**?

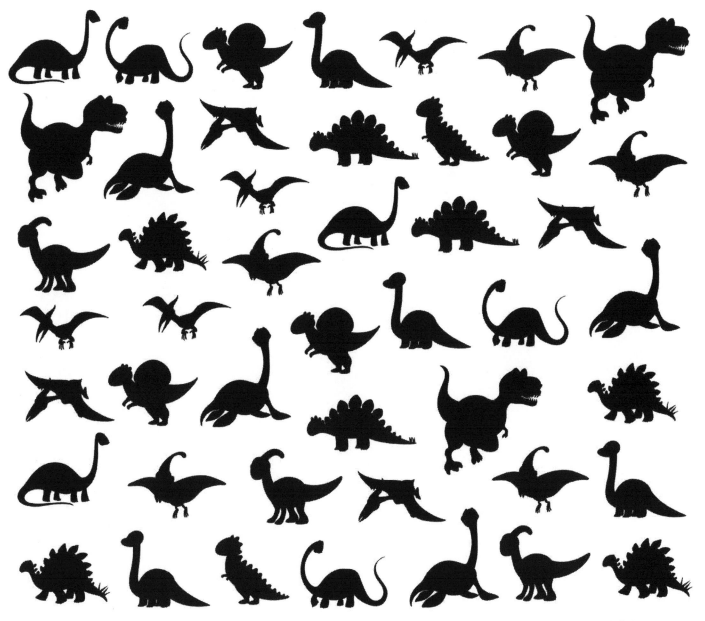

AND WHICH SHADOW APPEARS THE **LEAST**?

FIND MY FRIEND!

She's lost in a really tricky maze!

DINOSAURS

ANSWERS!

MISSING T-REX

T R X E X **X** R E T X T R X E
E T R E T **X** E R E T X R E X
R T X E E T **E** R X T E E R T
T X E R X T R **R** T E X T R E
X E R E X T X T **T** T X E X R
T E R X T E E X E R R X E T
T R X E T R X X T E X R E X
X T E R E R T E R E X E T E

OH NO... VOLCANO!

WHICH DINOSAUR IS WHICH?

VELOCIRAPTOR   DEINONYCHUS

IGUANODON   ANKYLOSAURUS   PTERANODON

BRACHIOSAURUS   ALLOSAURUS   PLESIOSAURUS

ALL THINGS DINOSAUR!

T	T	W	I	N	G	S	P	C	I	C	H	A	S
C	T	N	H	R	E	R	I	V	I	W	I	I	E
N	G	R	P	S	E	R	T	N	A	I	G	R	L
I	T	O	T	D	A	C	O	J	C	C	O	A	A
T	A	T	A	P	T	S	U	V	S	L	I	A	C
X	H	T	T	U	R	G	R	I	G	A	N	S	S
E	O	O	H	I	A	A	S	G	C	B	W	W	E
R	R	P	A	S	C	O	I	N	E	C	R	T	S
A	A	E	S	P	I	R	A	O	R	T	R	E	G
O	G	I	E	N	R	S	S	E	P	O	E	E	H
O	C	L	I	S	S	O	F	T	R	I	H	A	A
R	P	R	E	H	I	S	T	O	R	I	C	R	P
W	O	G	S	F	S	A	A	I	O	A	A	S	S
I	W	E	O	S	C	O	H	A	O	L	O	C	O

THE TASTIEST TREE!

SCRAMBLED!

Can you unscramble the dinosaur names?

ALLOSAURUS

DIPLODOCUS

BARYONYX

CARNOTAURUS

IGUANODON

TRICERATOPS

TRACHODON

TYPES OF DINOSAUR!

D	I	P	L	O	D	O	C	U	S	E	T	X	A
S	G	X	O	U	R	A	S	S	T	R	Y	R	S
T	U	Y	A	S	D	O	X	I	I	R	O	P	U
E	A	N	N	U	N	S	A	C	E	T	R	A	R
G	N	O	S	P	P	A	E	T	P	A	I	L	U
O	O	D	G	R	O	R	P	A	O	A	T	L	A
S	D	R	U	R	A	O	R	L	O	D	O	O	S
A	O	A	R	T	E	I	R	U	G	O	P	S	O
U	N	A	O	A	C	S	A	R	G	S	C	A	T
R	A	P	H	O	U	O	P	P	T	O	V	U	A
U	S	C	L	A	O	R	P	O	U	D	U	R	P
S	R	E	O	P	R	G	O	Y	O	R	X	U	A
A	V	S	U	R	U	A	S	O	N	I	P	S	C
P	N	O	R	G	I	R	A	U	X	R	O	N	R

THE SHADOWS WITHOUT A DINOSAUR

WHICH **DINOSAUR** GETS TO MEET **THEIR TWIN?** =

DODGE THE **COMET!**

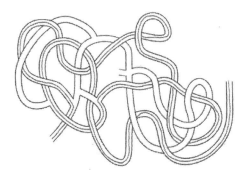

Count the dinosaurs
= 75

Count the dinosaur eggs
= 67

A DINOSAUR HAS BEEN CAUGHT STAMPING ON SOMEONE'S HOUSE!

CAN YOU SPOT THE FOOT PRINT LOCATED AT THE SCENE OF THE CRIME?

☐ ☐ ◼ ☐ ☐

WHICH SHADOW APPEARS THE **MOST...**

AND WHICH APPEARS THE **LEAST?**

FIND MY PARENTS!

TRICERATOPS   ANDESAURUS   STEGOSAURUS

SPINOSAURUS   TYRANNOSAURUS

WHICH **DINOSAUR** IS WHICH?

DIPLODOCUS   PARASAUROLOPHUS   HYPSILOPHODON

NAMES FOR DINOSAURS!

E	T	A	Y	R	M	O	E	R	H	S	A	T	B
G	C	M	S	E	E	T	R	P	T	Y	R	E	A
X	H	S	R	T	T	O	Y	R	O	R	Y	T	E
E	O	T	R	S	E	I	D	R	R	Y	R	N	S
I	M	N	E	E	H	G	B	R	O	I	T	Y	R
I	P	O	X	R	R	A	G	I	K	N	G	Y	A
S	U	E	G	R	T	I	M	E	X	R	E	O	S
P	S	M	L	R	O	X	Y	M	R	C	E	R	E
I	R	D	K	I	I	C	R	G	E	S	D	I	I
W	H	S	A	D	B	M	Y	S	D	R	W	B	P
E	T	T	P	R	Y	R	L	A	N	Y	I	T	H
D	A	R	O	T	P	A	R	E	R	E	N	R	R
S	E	Y	S	H	P	Y	E	R	Y	A	A	K	O
R	I	A	N	K	R	B	G	K	M	I	T	M	R

EGG HUNT!

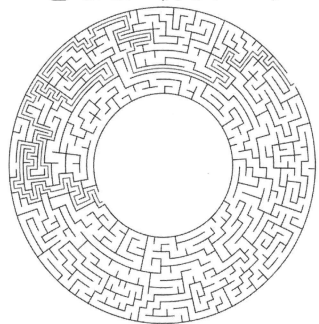

WHICH DINOSAUR SHADOW APPEARS THE **MOST**?

AND WHICH SHADOW APPEARS THE **LEAST**?

FIND MY FRIEND!

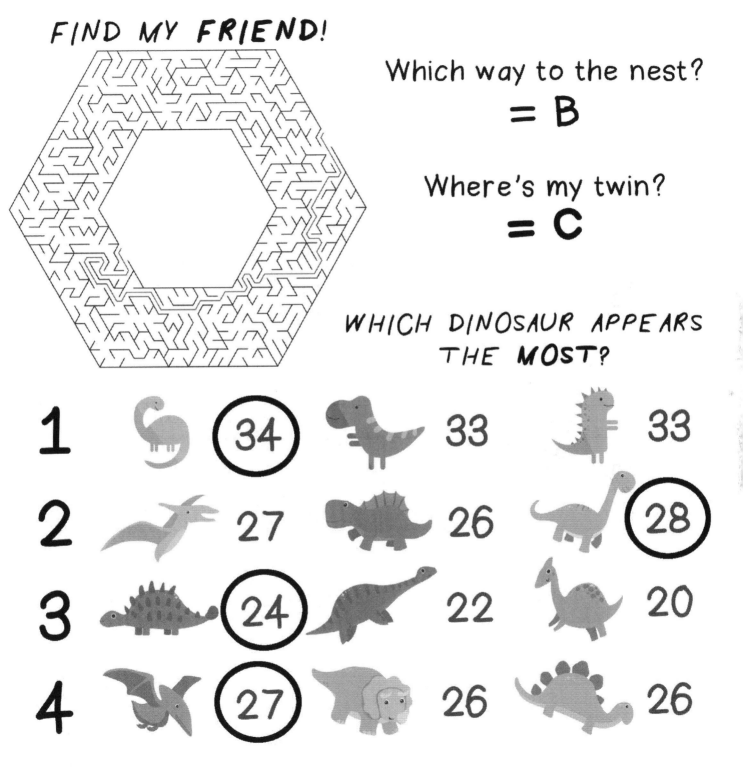

Which way to the nest?
= B

Where's my twin?
= C

WHICH DINOSAUR APPEARS THE MOST?

1   34   33   33

2   27   26   28

3   24   22   20

4   27   26   26

OTHER ACTIVITY BOOKS ALSO AVAILABLE!

CATS, KITTENS AND CATS!

DOGS, PUPPIES AND DOGS!

BIRDS, OWLS AND BIRDS!

BUGS, SPIDERS AND INSECTS!

FISH, DOLPHINS AND FISH!

ANIMALS IN THE WILD!

ANIMALS ON THE FARM!

HAPPY HALLOWEEN!

MERRY CHRISTMAS!

SUPERHEROES!

Printed in Poland
by Amazon Fulfillment
Poland Sp. z o.o., Wrocław

55022411R00040